D0118939

Special Days

A record keeper for birthdays, anniversaries & special days

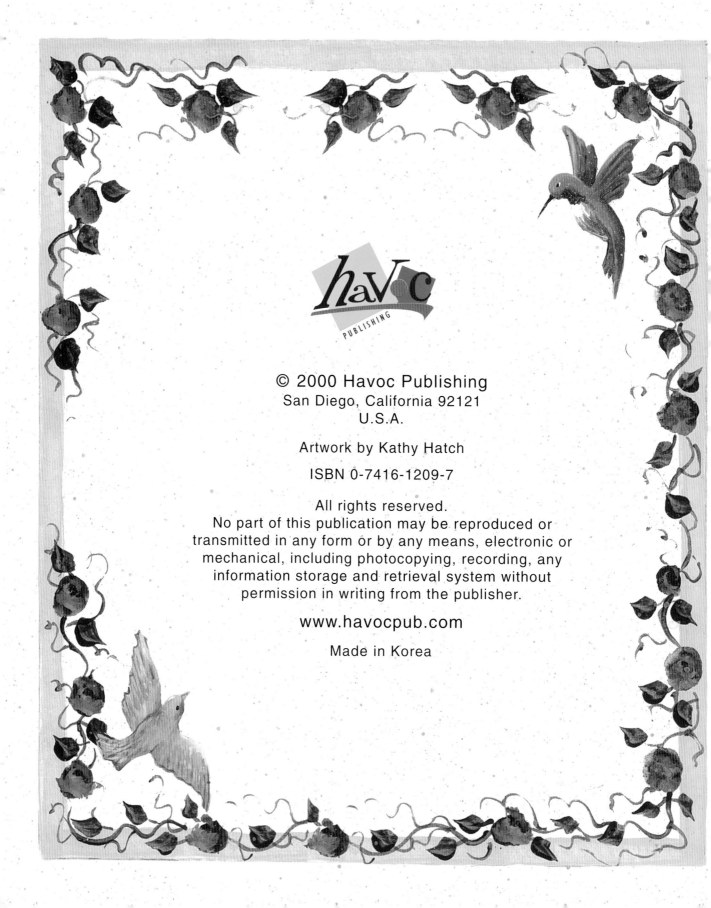

© 2000 Havoc Publishing
San Diego, California 92121
U.S.A.

Artwork by Kathy Hatch

ISBN 0-7416-1209-7

All rights reserved.
No part of this publication may be reproduced or
transmitted in any form or by any means, electronic or
mechanical, including photocopying, recording, any
information storage and retrieval system without
permission in writing from the publisher.

www.havocpub.com

Made in Korea

This book belongs to:

_____

There is no season such delight can bring,
As summer, autumn, winter and the spring.

William Browne

January

HOPE

FAITH

FRIENDS

FAMILY

LIGHT FADES.... STARS APPEAR

EVENING ANGELS.... GATHER HERE

EVENING ANGELS.... GATHER HERE

JOY

friends

HOPE

LOVE

FAITH

Family

PEACE

LOVE

LIGHT FADES.... STARS APPEAR

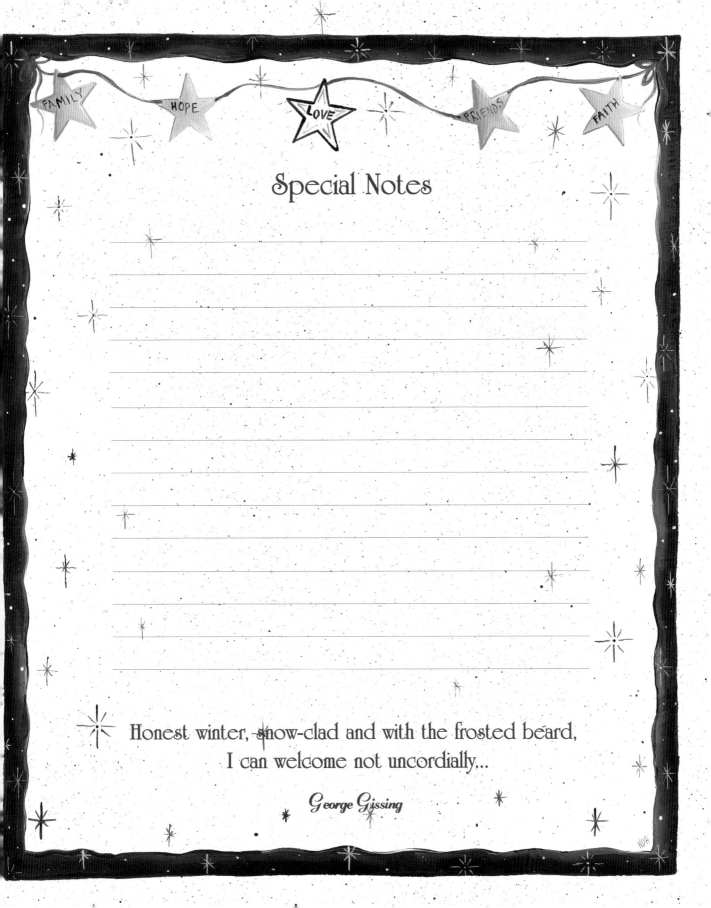

Special Notes

Honest winter, snow-clad and with the frosted beard,
I can welcome not uncordially...

George Gissing

FAMILY HOPE LOVE FRIENDS FAITH

January

1 _____
_____
_____

2 _____
_____
_____

3 _____
_____

4 _____
_____

5 _____
_____
_____

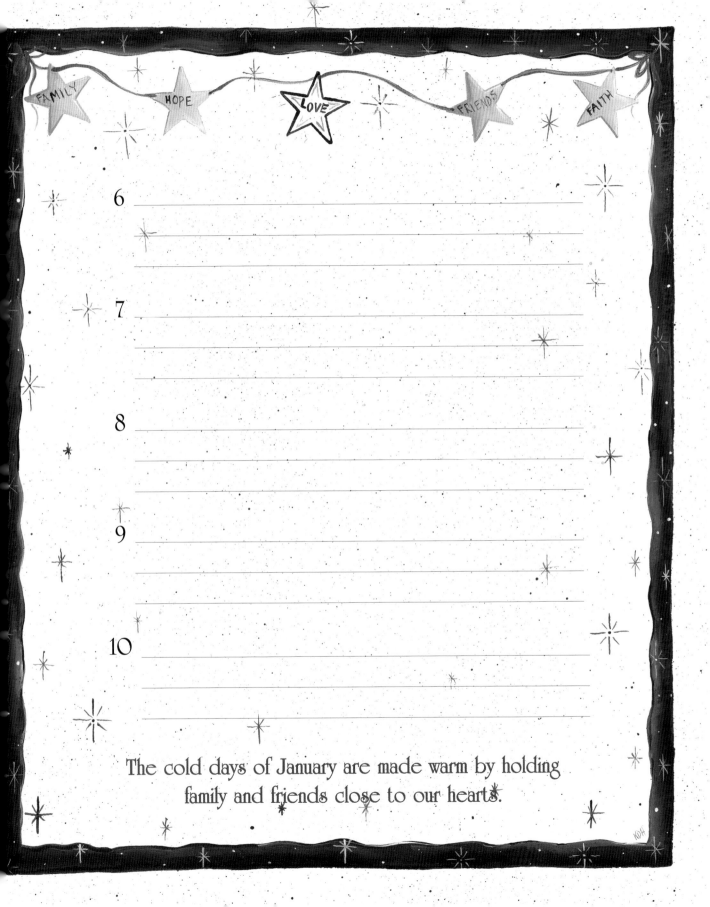

FAMILY   HOPE   LOVE   FRIENDS   FAITH

6 _____
_____
_____

7 _____
_____
_____

8 _____
_____
_____

9 _____
_____
_____

10 _____
_____
_____

The cold days of January are made warm by holding
family and friends close to our hearts.

January

11 _____
_____
_____

12 _____
_____
_____

13 _____
_____
_____

14 _____
_____
_____

15 _____
_____
_____

16

17

18

19

20

FAMILY HOPE LOVE FRIENDS FAITH

We do not see nature with our eyes,
but with our understandings and our hearts.

William Hazlitt

21 _____

_____

_____

22 _____

_____

_____

23 _____

_____

_____

24 _____

_____

_____

25 _____

_____

_____

FAMILY
HOPE
LOVE
FRIENDS
FAITH

January

26

27

28

29

30/31

February

Special Notes

We do not often stop to thank those who do the
most for us. Let us take some time each
day to reflect upon the love of
our friends, and to return this love in kind.

February

1 _____
_____
_____

2 _____
_____
_____

3 _____
_____
_____

4 _____
_____
_____

5 _____
_____
_____

6 _____

7 _____

8 _____

9 _____

10 _____

Let us love winter, for it is the spring of genius.

Pietro Aretino

February

11 _____

_____

_____

12 _____

_____

_____

13 _____

_____

_____

14 _____

_____

_____

15 _____

_____

16 _____
_____
_____

17 _____
_____
_____

18 _____
_____
_____

19 _____
_____
_____

20 _____
_____
_____

February

21 _____
_____
_____

22 _____
_____
_____

23 _____
_____
_____

24 _____
_____
_____

25 _____
_____
_____

26 _____

_____

_____

27 _____

_____

_____

28 _____

_____

_____

29 _____

_____

_____

February is a time to let all the
important people in your life know
how much you love them.

Special Notes

In our hearts, those of us who know anything worth knowing know that in March a new year begins, and if we plan any new leaves, it will be when the rest of Nature is planning them too.

Joseph Wood Krutch

March

1 _____
  _____
  _____

2 _____
  _____
  _____

3 _____
  _____
  _____

4 _____
  _____

5 _____
  _____
  _____

Daffodils,
that come before the swallow dares, and take
the winds of March with beauty. *Shakespeare*

6 _____

_____

_____

7 _____

_____

_____

8 _____

_____

_____

9 _____

_____

_____

10 _____

_____

_____

March

11 _____

_____

_____

12 _____

_____

_____

13 _____

_____

_____

14 _____

_____

_____

15 _____

_____

_____

16

17

18

19

20

The winds of March blow happiness and joy into our lives when they bring news of those who are dear.

21 _____

_____

_____

22 _____

_____

_____

23 _____

_____

_____

24 _____

_____

_____

25 _____

_____

_____

March

26

27

28

29

30/31

Special Notes

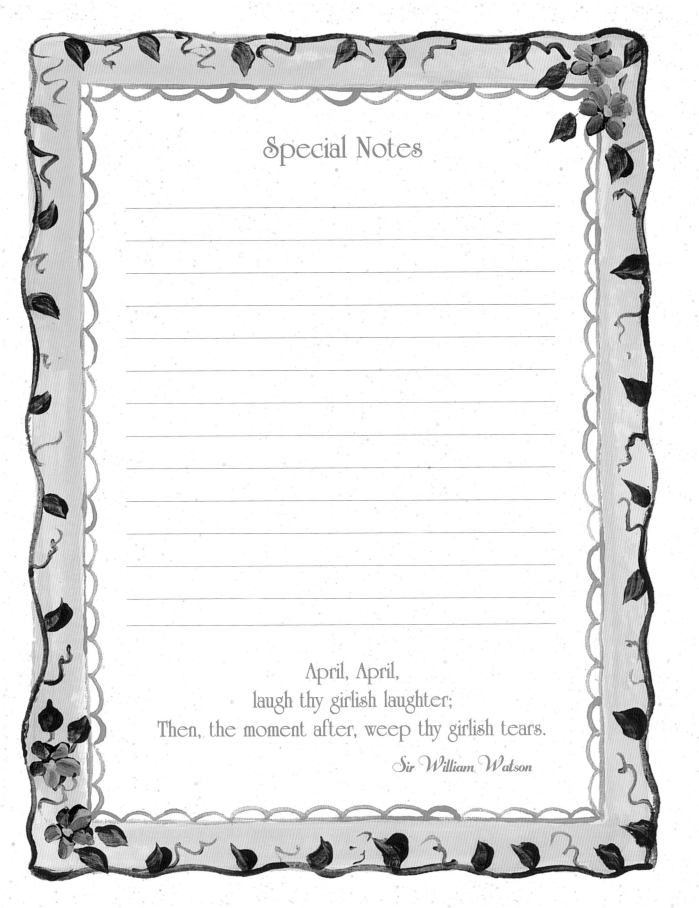

April, April,
laugh thy girlish laughter;
Then, the moment after, weep thy girlish tears.

Sir William Watson

April

1

2

3

4

5

6 _____

_____

_____

7 _____

_____

_____

8 _____

_____

_____

9 _____

_____

_____

10 _____

_____

_____

April is a time for planning a spring filled with special
days spent with family and friends.

April

11

12

13

14

15

16 _____

_____

_____

17 _____

_____

_____

18 _____

_____

_____

19 _____

_____

_____

20 _____

_____

_____

Spring is never spring unless it comes too soon.

G. K. Chesterton

April

21 _____
_____
_____

22 _____
_____
_____

23 _____
_____
_____

24 _____
_____
_____

25 _____
_____
_____

26 _____
_____
_____

27 _____
_____
_____

28 _____
_____
_____

29 _____
_____
_____

30 _____
_____
_____

O! how this spring resembleth
the uncertain glory of an April day!

Shakespeare

Apple Tree

Gate

Fence

Pear Tree

Red Roses

Stone Walkway

Dogwood

Garden Bench

Lavender

Stepping Stones

Fish Pond

Water Lilies

Day Lilies

Gate

Silver Mound

Veronica

Red Roses

Day Lilies

Pear Tree

May

WELCOME

WELCOME TO MY GARDEN

KDH

Special Notes

"I know a little garden close, set thick
with lily and red rose, where I might wander if I might
from dewy morn to dewy night."

William Morris

May

1 _____
_____
_____

2 _____
_____
_____

3 _____
_____
_____

4 _____
_____
_____

5 _____
_____

The world's favorite season is the spring.
All things seem popular in May.
Edwin Way Teale

6 _____

_____

_____

7 _____

_____

_____

8 _____

_____

_____

9 _____

_____

_____

10 _____

_____

_____

May

11

12

13

14

15

16 _____

_____

_____

17 _____

_____

_____

18 _____

_____

_____

19 _____

_____

_____

20 _____

_____

_____

May brings sunshine and flowers to our lives as
do close friends and family.

Flowers create a happy mood.
With cheerful faces they shape a blissful attitude.
That's why gardens are happy places.

'21 _____
_____
_____

'22 _____
_____
_____

'23 _____
_____
_____

'24 _____
_____
_____

'25 _____
_____
_____

May

26

27

28

29

30/31

ZINNIA SEEDS

MORNING GLORY

ANNUAL

NET WT 4 OZ

ANTIQUE SEEDS

June

Perennials

Annuals

Bulbs

DRIED FLOWERS

Special Notes

And what is so rare as a day in June?
Then, if ever, come perfect days.

James Russell Lowell

June

1

2

3

4

5

6 _____

_____

_____

7 _____

_____

_____

8 _____

_____

_____

9 _____

_____

_____

10 _____

_____

O, my love is like a red, red rose,
that's newly sprung in June.

Robert Burns

June

11

12

13

14

15

16

17

18

19

20

June

21 _____
_____
_____

22 _____
_____
_____

23 _____
_____
_____

24 _____
_____
_____

25 _____
_____
_____

26 _____
  _____
  _____

27 _____
  _____
  _____

28 _____
  _____
  _____

29 _____
  _____
  _____

30 _____
  _____
  _____

June, a month filled with bright days
and smiling faces,
a time to laugh with friends
and play with family.

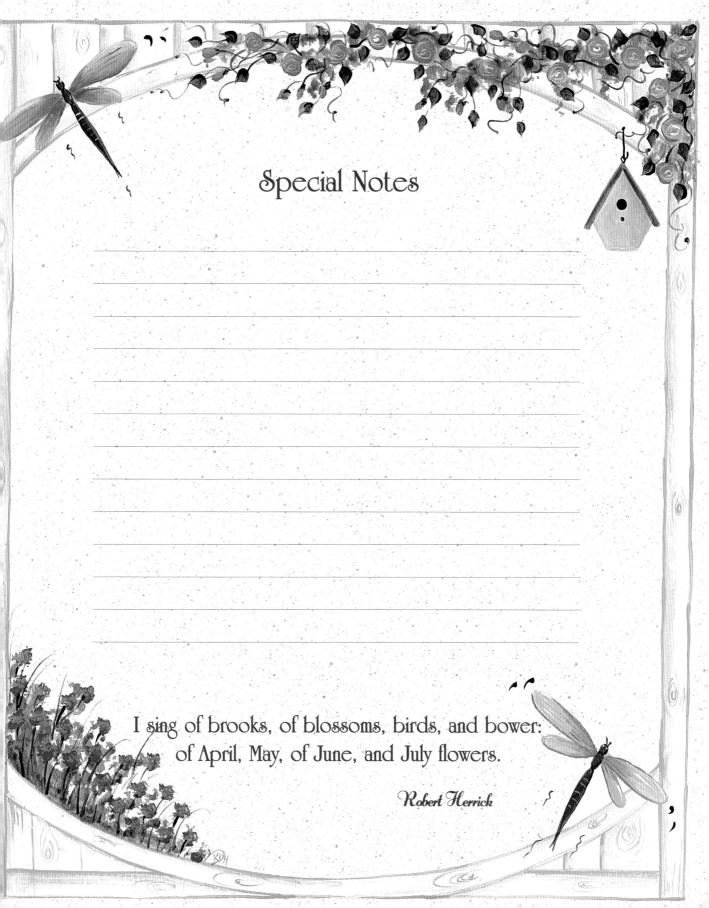

Special Notes

I sing of brooks, of blossoms, birds, and bower:
of April, May, of June, and July flowers.

Robert Herrick

July

1 _____
_____
_____

2 _____
_____
_____

3 _____
_____
_____

4 _____
_____
_____

5 _____
_____
_____

6 _____

_____

_____

7 _____

_____

_____

8 _____

_____

_____

9 _____

_____

_____

10 _____

_____

_____

July

11 _____

_____

_____

12 _____

_____

_____

13 _____

_____

_____

14 _____

_____

_____

15 _____

_____

_____

16 _____

_____

_____

17 _____

_____

_____

18 _____

_____

_____

19 _____

_____

_____

20 _____

_____

_____

I should like to enjoy this summer
flower by flower, as if it were to be
the last one for me.

Andre Gide

July

21

22

23

24

25

26 _____

_____

_____

27 _____

_____

_____

28 _____

_____

_____

29 _____

_____

_____

30/31 _____

_____

_____

Let the warmth of the sun in
July warm your soul as time spent with
loved ones does.

Bee-Balm for hummingbirds, roses for the bee. Berries for the wild birds and hollyhocks for me!

August

Special Notes

_____

_____

_____

_____

_____

_____

_____

_____

_____

_____

_____

August creates as she slumbers,
replete and satisfied.

Joseph Wood Krutch

August

1

2

3

4

5

6 _____

_____

_____

7 _____

_____

_____

8 _____

_____

_____

9 _____

_____

_____

10 _____

_____

_____

August

11

12

13

14

15

16 _____

_____

_____

17 _____

_____

_____

18 _____

_____

_____

19 _____

_____

_____

20 _____

_____

_____

The leaves fall early this autumn, in the wind. The paired
butterflies are already yellow with August.

Ezra Pound

August

21 _____

_____

_____

22 _____

_____

_____

23 _____

_____

_____

24 _____

_____

_____

25 _____

_____

_____

26 _____

_____

_____

27 _____

_____

_____

28 _____

_____

_____

29 _____

_____

_____

30/31 _____

_____

_____

August is a time for watching the leaves
turn and fall, a time to gather close to us
those that make our lives complete.

Special Notes

_____

_____

_____

_____

_____

_____

_____

_____

_____

_____

_____

_____

_____

_____

For man autumn is a time of harvest, of gathering together.
For nature, it is a time of sowing, of scattering abroad.

Edwin Way Teale

September

1 _____
_____
_____

2 _____
_____
_____

3 _____
_____
_____

4 _____
_____
_____

5 _____
_____
_____

6 _____

_____

_____

7 _____

_____

_____

8 _____

_____

_____

9 _____

_____

_____

10 _____

_____

_____

Gardening involves its own traditions. There is a
certain time to plant, to reap and be grateful
for the bounty of the harvest.

September

11 _____

_____

_____

12 _____

_____

_____

13 _____

_____

_____

14 _____

_____

_____

15 _____

_____

_____

16 _____
_____
_____

17 _____
_____
_____

18 _____
_____
_____

19 _____
_____
_____

20 _____
_____
_____

Up from the meadows rich with corn,
Clear the cool September morn.

John Greenleaf Whittier

September

21 _____

_____

_____

22 _____

_____

_____

23 _____

_____

_____

24 _____

_____

_____

25 _____

_____

_____

26 _____

_____

_____

27 _____

_____

_____

28 _____

_____

_____

29 _____

_____

_____

30 _____

_____

_____

September is a time to show all those who
are special in our lives that we love them.

Special Notes

October is the fallen leaf, but it is also
a wider horizon more clearly seen.

Hal Borland

October

1 _____

_____

_____

2 _____

_____

_____

3 _____

_____

_____

4 _____

_____

_____

5 _____

_____

_____

6 _____

_____

_____

7 _____

_____

_____

8 _____

_____

_____

9 _____

_____

_____

10 _____

_____

_____

October

11

12

13

14

15

16

17

18

19

20

October

21

22

23

24

25

26

27

28

29

30/31

October is a time for harvesting the love and care
that has been sown throughout the year.

Special Notes

When it turns cold outside;
as happens in November,
it is time to gather close to us
those that bring to our lives warmth.

November

1 _____

_____

_____

2 _____

_____

_____

3 _____

_____

_____

4 _____

_____

_____

5 _____

_____

_____

November's sky is chill and drear,
November's leaf is red and sear. *Sir Walter Scott*

6 _____

_____

_____

7 _____

_____

_____

8 _____

_____

_____

9 _____

_____

_____

10 _____

_____

_____

November

11 _____
_____
_____

12 _____
_____
_____

13 _____
_____
_____

14 _____
_____
_____

15 _____
_____
_____

16 _____

_____

_____

17 _____

_____

_____

18 _____

_____

_____

19 _____

_____

_____

20 _____

_____

_____

November

21 _____
_____
_____

22 _____
_____
_____

23 _____
_____
_____

24 _____
_____
_____

25 _____
_____
_____

For you there's rosemary and rue: these keep
Seeming and savor all the winter long.   *Shakespeare*

26 _____

_____

_____

27 _____

_____

_____

28 _____

_____

_____

29 _____

_____

_____

30 _____

_____

_____

Special Notes

I shall love you in December
With the love I gave in May!

John Alexander Joyce

December

1 _____
_____
_____

2 _____
_____
_____

3 _____
_____
_____

4 _____
_____
_____

5 _____
_____
_____

6 _____

_____

_____

7 _____

_____

_____

8 _____

_____

_____

9 _____

_____

_____

10 _____

_____

_____

O Wind, if winter comes,
can spring be far behind?

Percy Bysshe Shelley

December

11 _____

12 _____

13 _____

14 _____

15 _____

16 _____

17 _____

18 _____

19 _____

20 _____

December

21

22

23

24

25

December, a time
for giving and sharing
our love and joy.

26 _____

27 _____

28 _____

29 _____

30/31 _____

Thirty days hath November, April, June and September,
February hath twenty-eight alone,
And all the rest have thirty-one.

Richard Grafton

with
Warm Wishes!

Kathy Natch